EFFO CA PROTEIN LOW-CARB DIET FOR WEIGHT LOSS

Healthy Way To lose Weight with 1200 Calorie Meal Plan With Delicious Low Carb High Protein Recipes . (+ 28 weeks Meal Planner.)

MITCHELL OLIVIA

COPYRIGHT

Copyright © 2024 [**MITCHELL OLIVIA**]

All rights reserved. No part of this publication may be reproduced, distributed, or transmitted in any form or by any means, including photocopying, recording, or other electronic or mechanical methods, without the prior written permission of the publisher, except in the case of brief quotations embodied in critical reviews and certain other noncommercial uses permitted by copyright law.

Contents

INTRODUCTION

Tired of feeling trapped in a cycle of restrictive diets and disappointing results? Longing for delicious meals that actually help you shed pounds? Consider this book your key to unlocking healthy weight loss without sacrificing flavor or fun.

Forget everything you thought about bland, boring "diet food." This isn't about deprivation. It's about empowerment. Inside these pages, you'll discover a treasure trove of easy, mouthwatering recipes designed by a leading dietitian with over 20 years of experience. Each dish is a symphony of high-protein, low-carb goodness that your taste buds will sing about, while your body celebrates with sustainable, healthy weight loss.

Here's just a taste of what awaits:

- **Effortless breakfasts** that kickstart your day without the guilt. Imagine fluffy protein pancakes drizzled with berry sauce, or a savory frittata bursting with fresh veggies.
- **Lunchtime** salads that transform from boring to bold and beautiful. Think grilled chicken with a creamy avocado dressing or a shrimp scampi salad bursting with citrusy flavor.

- **Dinners** that wow without the "diet" label. Indulge in tender salmon glazed with a honey-Dijon sauce or juicy steak fajitas served with all the trimmings.
- **Satisfying snacks** that keep you on track, not tempted. Ditch the chips and dip for roasted pumpkin seeds packed with protein and healthy fats, or whip up a creamy cauliflower soup for a cozy, low-carb treat.

This isn't just a cookbook; it's a roadmap to a healthier, happier you. We'll guide you through every step, from stocking your pantry with the right ingredients to mastering essential cooking techniques. You'll also discover:

- Clear, concise information about low-carb eating, its benefits, and potential challenges.
- Expert tips and tricks for meal planning, prepping, and conquering common hurdles.
- Motivational anecdotes and success stories to keep you inspired on your journey.

Stop dreaming about weight loss and start achieving it. With **"Easy Low Calorie, High Protein, Low-Carb Diet,"** you'll unlock a world of delicious possibilities, where healthy eating and sustainable weight loss go hand in hand. This isn't just a cookbook; it's your passport to a healthier, happier, and more confident you. Ready to get started? **Let's go!**

CHAPTER 1

Understanding Low-Calorie, High-Protein, Low-Carb Eating

Raise your hand if you're tired of the diet roller coaster. Restrictive plans, bland food, and the ever-present feeling of missing out – yeah, it gets old. But **what if there was a different way?** What if losing weight could involve bursting flavors, satisfying meals, and feeling genuinely empowered? Enter the world of low-calorie, high-protein, low-carb eating.

Now, before you roll your eyes at the word **"diet,"** hold on. **This isn't about deprivation or feeling hungry**. This is about shifting your approach to food in a way that supports your weight loss goals while treating your taste buds to a celebration.

Let's break it down:

1. **Low-calorie:** We're not talking starvation mode here. It's about creating a slight calorie deficit to encourage your body to burn stored fat for energy. But worry not, the recipes in this book will keep you feeling full and satisfied.

2. **High-protein:** Protein is your weight loss bestie. It keeps you feeling fuller for longer, boosts your metabolism, and

even helps build and maintain muscle, which burns more calories at rest. So, prepare to say hello to protein powerhouses like lean meats, fish, eggs, and legumes.

3. **Low-carb**: Here's where things get interesting. By limiting sugary and starchy carbs, we help regulate blood sugar, reduce cravings, and encourage the body to use fat for fuel. But don't worry, we're not ditching all carbs – just the refined, processed ones. Think colorful veggies, nuts, and seeds to keep your taste buds happy and your body on track.

But why go down this path? The benefits are pretty sweet:

- **Sustainable weight loss:** This isn't a fad diet. It's a sustainable approach that helps you develop healthy habits you can stick with for the long haul.
- **Improved energy levels:** Say goodbye to afternoon slumps. This combination of protein and healthy fats fuels your body and mind for lasting energy.
- **Reduced cravings:** No more sugar highs and crashes. By stabilizing blood sugar, you'll experience fewer cravings and make healthier choices naturally.
- **Overall health boost:** Studies suggest this approach can improve heart health, manage blood sugar, and even reduce the risk of chronic diseases.

Does it meet your needs? Sit up, for this book will show you the ropes when it comes to the thrilling realm of nutritious eating. We will explore the science in more detail, debunk common misconceptions, and, most importantly, give you a collection of recipes that are far from boring. This isn't about starving yourself; rather, it's about re-discovering the pleasure of eating nutritious, tasty food that nourishes your body and soul.

Consequently, I say we set out on this adventure together. **Low-calorie, high-protein, low-carb food** has incredible potential; let's stop depriving ourselves and start enjoying it. It is time to feel great on the inside and out, and this book will show you how to do just that.

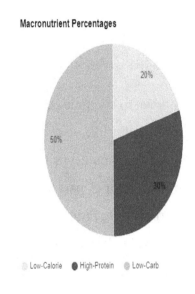

Macronutrient Percentages

Low-Calorie ● High-Protein ● Low-Carb

Understanding the science behind this approach for weight loss.

We've talked about the delicious possibilities of low-calorie, high-protein, low-carb eating, but let's peel back the onion and explore the science behind this winning weight-loss combo. Buckle up, because we're about to get nerdy – in the best way possible!

Energy In, Energy Out: The Calorie Equation

At its core, weight loss boils down to a simple equation: burn more calories than you consume. It's like your body's a bank account – when you spend more than you deposit, you lose weight (fat stores). That's where the "low-calorie" part comes in. This approach creates a gentle calorie deficit, prompting your body to dip into its fat reserves for energy, leading to the happy consequence of shedding pounds. But it's not just about cutting calories; it's about the quality of those calories.

Protein: The Satiety Superhero

Enter protein, your weight-loss BFF. Unlike carbs, which can cause blood sugar spikes and crashes, protein keeps you feeling fuller for longer. Why? It takes longer to digest and absorb, sending signals to your brain that say "Hey, I'm satisfied, thanks!" This translates to fewer cravings and less mindless snacking – a major win for your weight-loss goals. Plus, protein helps build and maintain muscle, which burns more calories at rest, even when you're chilling on the couch (score!).

Carbs: Not All Created Equal

Now, let's talk carbs. They get a bad rap sometimes, but here's the deal: carbs provide energy, and certain types are crucial for good health. However, refined carbs like white bread, sugary drinks, and pastries can cause blood sugar spikes and crashes, leaving you feeling hungry and cranky. That's where the "low-carb" part comes in.

By limiting these refined carbs, we help stabilize blood sugar, reduce cravings, and encourage the body to use fat for fuel – another step closer to your weight-loss goals. But fear not, we're not talking about ditching all carbs! We'll focus on nutrient-rich options like colorful veggies, nuts, and seeds to keep you energized and feeling your best.

The Hormonal Symphony: Insulin and the Fat-Burning Dance

Here's where things get even more fascinating. Carbs, especially refined ones, trigger the release of insulin, a hormone that helps your body store energy as fat. By limiting these carbs, we keep insulin levels lower, creating an environment more conducive to fat burning. It's like conducting a hormonal orchestra, orchestrating a symphony of fat-burning magic!

But Wait, There's More!

The benefits of this approach extend beyond just weight loss. Studies suggest it can improve heart health, manage blood sugar, and even reduce the risk of chronic diseases like type 2 diabetes. Pretty impressive, right?

Science is complex, but the takeaway is simple: Low-calorie, high-protein, low-carb eating creates a powerful formula for weight loss by managing calories, harnessing the power of protein, and optimizing your body's fat-burning potential. Now that you've got the science under your belt, let's put it into action with the delicious recipes in this book. Prepare to experience the joy of healthy eating and unlock your amazing weight-loss potential.

Setting realistic expectations and goals.

Let's talk goals. You've decided to embark on this low-calorie, high-protein, low-carb journey, and excitement (and maybe a touch of trepidation) is buzzing in your veins. But hold on to your horses before you start picturing yourself at your dream weight next week. Sustainable weight loss is a marathon, not a sprint. So, let's set some realistic expectations and goals that'll propel you forward with joy, not frustration.

Do away with the **"get-skinny-quick"** attitude immediately. It seems good in theory, but in practice, it's usually not feasible. Although it may not sound as exciting, the secret to long-term success is to aim for healthy, steady weight loss, which should not exceed one to two pounds per week. This is similar to laying a solid foundation for a house: it must be done slowly and steadily if the house is to last.

Now, let's get specific with your goals. Don't just say "lose weight." Instead, craft SMART goals: Specific, Measurable, Achievable, Relevant, and Time-bound. For example, "I will replace sugary drinks with water for the next month, aiming to lose

4 pounds." See the difference? It's clear, trackable, and achievable, boosting your motivation and setting you up for success.

Keep in mind that progress isn't necessarily in a direct path. There will be ups and downs, challenges, and maybe even the occasional cupcake binge are all part of the journey. We expect it! Stay focused and determined. Stay positive, keep your eye on the prize, and reward yourself when you reach milestones along the way. Always keep in mind that this is a trip and not a mission of retribution.

Here are some tips to keep your expectations realistic and your goals attainable:

- Focus on healthy habits, not just weight loss. Building sustainable habits like mindful eating, reading food labels, and planning meals is key to long-term success.
- Find an accountability partner or support group. Share your journey with someone who understands and cheers you on.
- Don't compare yourself to others. Everyone's body and journey are unique. Focus on your own progress and celebrate your individuality.
- Embrace flexibility. Life happens! A missed workout or an occasional treat doesn't derail your progress. Get back on track and move forward.

- Enjoy the process. Discover new foods, experiment in the kitchen, and savor the deliciousness of healthy eating.

This journey is about more than just a number on the scale. It's about feeling energized, confident, and empowered in your own skin. So, set realistic expectations, celebrate small wins, and most importantly, **enjoy the ride!** This book is your roadmap, packed with delicious recipes and valuable information to support you every step of the way. Let's embark on this journey together, embrace the marathon mindset, and unlock your healthiest ansd happiest self.

An individual's weight is only one small part of this journey. Having a sense of vitality, **self-assurance, and strength is key.** The most important thing is to have fun, establish reasonable goals, and reward yourself when you succeed. Here you will find helpful instructions, tasty recipes, and insightful data to guide you on your journey. Join me as we take this next step toward realizing your healthiest, happiest self by adopting a "marathon mindset."

CHAPTER 2

Essential Nutrients for Weight Loss and Overall Health

Remember that fancy car you saw with a sleek design and powerful engine? It wouldn't go far without the right fuel, would it? Well, guess what? Your body is kind of like that car, and food is your fuel. But unlike your car, your body needs a diverse range of nutrients, not just one type of gas. So, buckle up, because in this chapter, we'll explore the world of essential nutrients, understanding how they power your weight loss journey and overall health.

Think of nutrients as the building blocks of life. They keep your energy levels high, your mind sharp, and your body functioning optimally. But in the context of weight loss, understanding specific nutrients becomes even more crucial.

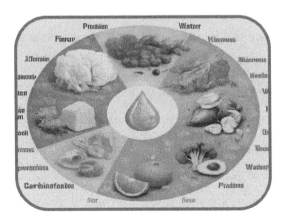

Ensuring dietary adequacy on a low-carb plan.

Let's face it, exploring a low-carb world can feel daunting. Worries about missing out on essential nutrients might linger on the back of your mind. But fear not, fellow adventurer. This section equips you with the knowledge and tools to ensure your low-carb journey is not just weight-loss focused, but also nutrient-rich and sustainable.

First things first, let's address the elephant in the room: yes, some low-carb plans can lead to nutrient deficiencies if not carefully planned. This is mainly because certain essential vitamins and minerals are primarily found in fruits, vegetables, and whole grains, which are often restricted on stricter low-carb approaches.

But hold on, don't panic! Here are some key strategies to ensure you're getting everything your body needs:

1. **Embrace the Rainbow:** Don't underestimate the power of low-carb veggies. Fill your plate with a variety of colorful vegetables like broccoli, peppers, leafy greens, and cauliflower. They're packed with vitamins, minerals, and fiber, keeping you feeling full and nourished.

2. **Don't Forget the Healthy Fats:** Avocados, nuts, seeds, and olive oil are your low-carb friends. They provide

essential fatty acids, support nutrient absorption, and contribute to satiety, keeping you off the "hangry" wagon.

3. **Choose Whole Foods Wisely:** Opt for whole grains like quinoa and brown rice in moderation. They offer valuable fiber, vitamins, and minerals compared to their refined counterparts.

4. **Supplement Strategically:** While food should be your primary source of nutrients, consider consulting your doctor about personalized supplementation. They can assess your individual needs and recommend options to fill any potential gaps.

5. **Prioritize Protein Power:** Lean meats, fish, eggs, and legumes are your protein powerhouses. They not only keep you feeling full but also provide essential vitamins and minerals like iron, zinc, and B vitamins.

6. **Read Food Labels Like a Detective:** Pay attention to the nutrient content of your food choices. Look for options fortified with vitamins and minerals, especially those commonly lacking in low-carb diets.

7. **Seek Professional Guidance:** A registered dietitian can personalize your low-carb plan to ensure it meets your individual needs and preferences. They can help you navigate potential deficiencies and create a balanced, sustainable approach.

Always keep variation in mind. Stay away from the same old boring low-carb foods. Discover tasty new ways to eat healthily by trying out new recipes and experimenting with different vegetables. You can lose weight and improve your health on a low-carb diet with some preparation and self-awareness.

On your journey to low-carb nutrition, this chapter will serve as your guide. By implementing the aforementioned tactics and, if necessary, consulting a healthcare provider, you may overcome concerns about carbohydrates, provide your body with the nourishment it needs, and enjoy the wonderful outcomes of a well-rounded approach to weight loss. Embrace the rainbow of low-carb options, get your metaphorical compass, and go out on a delightful adventure.

CHAPTER 3

Easy and Flavorful Breakfasts

Forget the same old bowl of cereal or rushed toast. Breakfast doesn't have to be boring or a hurried pitstop on your way out the door. It can be a flavorful fiesta, a protein-packed powerhouse, a sweet and satisfying symphony that sets the tone for a fantastic day. And guess what? It can be effortless to prepare, even on the busiest mornings.

This chapter is your ticket to breakfast bliss. We're getting rid of the bland and predictable, and diving into a world of easy, delicious recipes that will energize your body and tantalize your taste buds. No complicated ingredients, no fancy gadgets, just pure, simple culinary magic that anyone can whip up in a flash.

Whether you're a breakfast enthusiast or a time-pressed soul, this chapter has something for you. We'll guide you through each recipe with clear instructions and simple tips, ensuring success even for the most novice cook.

So, put down that stale cereal box and get ready to embark on a breakfast adventure. Explore the recipes, discover new flavors, and fuel your body and your spirit with deliciousness. It's time to make breakfast something you look forward to, not just endure. Let's get cookin'!

1. Egg White Omelette with Spinach and Tomato:

Ingredients:

- 2 large egg whites
- 1 tablespoon water
- Salt and pepper to taste
- 1/2 cup fresh spinach, chopped
- 1/4 cup diced tomato
- 1 tablespoon crumbled feta cheese (optional)
- Olive oil spray

Instructions:

- In a small bowl, whisk together egg whites and water until frothy. Season with salt and pepper.
- Heat a non-stick pan over medium heat and coat with olive oil spray. Pour in the egg white mixture and swirl the pan to create a thin layer.
- Let the omelette cook for 30 seconds, then add the spinach and tomatoes.
- Cook for another minute or until the egg whites are almost set.
- Sprinkle with feta cheese (optional) and fold the omelette in half.
- Slide onto a plate and enjoy!

2. Greek Yogurt with Granola and Berries:

Ingredients:

- 1 cup plain Greek yogurt
- 1/4 cup homemade low-carb granola (recipe below)
- 1/2 cup fresh berries of your choice

Instructions:

- Layer the Greek yogurt in a bowl.
- Top with homemade granola and fresh berries.
- Enjoy!

3. Homemade Low-Carb Granola:

Ingredients:

- 1 cup rolled almonds
- 1/2 cup chopped pecans
- 1/4 cup unsweetened shredded coconut
- 1/4 cup chia seeds
- 1 tablespoon melted coconut oil
- 1/4 teaspoon cinnamon
- Pinch of salt

Instructions:

- Preheat oven to 300°F.
- Combine all ingredients in a bowl and mix well.
- Spread onto a baking sheet and bake for 15-20 minutes, stirring occasionally, until golden brown and crispy.
- Let cool completely and store in an airtight container.

4. Almond Flour Pancakes with Sugar-Free Syrup:

Ingredients:

- 1/2 cup almond flour
- 1/4 teaspoon baking powder
- 1/4 teaspoon cinnamon
- Pinch of salt
- 1 large egg
- 1/4 cup unsweetened almond milk
- Olive oil spray
- Sugar-free syrup of your choice

Instructions:

- In a bowl, whisk together almond flour, baking powder, cinnamon, and salt.
- In a separate bowl, whisk together egg and almond milk.
- Combine the wet and dry ingredients until just combined, do not overmix.
- Heat a non-stick pan over medium heat and coat with olive oil spray.
- Pour 1/4 cup batter per pancake and cook for 2-3 minutes per side, or until golden brown.
- Serve with sugar-free syrup of your choice.

5. Turkey Bacon and Egg White Wrap:

Ingredients:

- 2 large egg whites
- Salt and pepper to taste
- 1 tablespoon diced onion
- 1 slice turkey bacon, cooked
- 1 low-carb tortilla
- Shredded lettuce (optional)
- Dijon mustard (optional)

Instructions:

- In a non-stick pan, cook egg whites with salt and pepper until scrambled.
- Add diced onion and cook for another minute.
- Warm low-carb tortilla in a microwave or pan.
- Spread Dijon mustard on the tortilla (optional).
- Add scrambled eggs, turkey bacon, and lettuce (optional).
- Fold and enjoy!

6. Chia Seed Pudding with Fresh Fruit:

Ingredients:

- 1/4 cup chia seeds
- 1 cup unsweetened almond milk
- 1 tablespoon maple syrup or honey (optional)
- 1/2 teaspoon vanilla extract
- Pinch of cinnamon
- 1/2 cup fresh fruit of your choice

Instructions:

- In a jar or bowl, combine chia seeds, almond milk, maple syrup (optional), vanilla extract, and cinnamon.
- Stir well and refrigerate overnight.
- In the morning, top with fresh fruit and enjoy!

7. Cottage Cheese and Fruit Salad:

Ingredients:

- 1/2 cup low-fat cottage cheese
- 1/2 cup mixed fruit of your choice
- 1 tablespoon chopped nuts (optional)
- Drizzle of honey (optional)

Instructions:

- In a bowl, combine cottage cheese and mixed fruit.
- Top with chopped nuts (optional).
- Drizzle with honey (optional) and enjoy!

8. Avocado Toast with a Poached Egg:

Ingredients:

- 1 slice whole-grain toast
- 1/2 avocado
- 1 poached egg
- Pinch of red pepper flakes (optional)
- Drizzle of lemon juice (optional)
- Salt and pepper to taste

Instructions:

- Toast the bread to your desired doneness.
- Mash the avocado and spread it on the toast.
- Poach an egg according to your preferred method. (Many methods exist, but boiling water with vinegar is a common choice.)
- Carefully place the poached egg on top of the avocado toast.
- Sprinkle with red pepper flakes (optional) and drizzle with lemon juice (optional).
- Season with salt and pepper to taste.
- Enjoy!

9. Spinach and Mushroom Frittata:

Ingredients:

- 8 large egg whites
- 1/4 cup milk of your choice
- 1 tablespoon olive oil
- 1/2 cup chopped spinach
- 1/4 cup sliced mushrooms
- 1/4 cup crumbled feta cheese (optional)
- Salt and pepper to taste

Instructions:

- Preheat oven to 375°F.
- Whisk together egg whites and milk in a large bowl. Season with salt and pepper.
- Heat olive oil in a large oven-safe skillet over medium heat.
- Add spinach and mushrooms and cook until softened, about 5 minutes.
- Pour in the egg white mixture and stir gently to combine.
- Sprinkle with feta cheese (optional) and bake in the preheated oven for 20-25 minutes, or until the frittata is set and golden brown.
- Let cool slightly before slicing and serving.

10. Protein Smoothie with Berries:

Ingredients:

- 1 scoop protein powder of your choice
- 1 cup unsweetened almond milk or other plant-based milk
- 1/2 cup spinach or kale
- 1/2 cup frozen berries of your choice
- 1/4 avocado (optional)
- 1/2 teaspoon ground cinnamon (optional)
- Ice cubes (optional)

Instructions:

- Combine all ingredients in a blender and blend until smooth and creamy.
- Add ice cubes (optional) for a thicker consistency.
- Enjoy!

11. Almond Flour Waffles with Greek Yogurt:

Ingredients:

- 1 cup almond flour
- 1/4 teaspoon baking powder
- 1/4 teaspoon baking soda
- Pinch of salt
- 1 large egg
- 1/2 cup unsweetened almond milk
- 1/4 cup unsweetened applesauce
- Olive oil spray
- Greek yogurt and fresh berries (for topping)

Instructions:

- In a bowl, whisk together almond flour, baking powder, baking soda, and salt.
- In a separate bowl, whisk together egg, almond milk, and applesauce.
- Combine the wet and dry ingredients until just combined, do not over mix.
- Heat a waffle iron according to manufacturer's instructions.
- Coat the waffle iron with olive oil spray.
- Pour batter into the waffle iron and cook for 3-4 minutes per side, or until golden brown and cooked through.

- Serve with Greek yogurt and fresh berries.

Tips:

- Feel free to adjust the sweetness of these recipes to your liking.
- Substitute ingredients based on your dietary preferences and allergies.
- Get creative and add your own personal touches to each recipe.

With these delicious and easy recipes, you can get rid of boring breakfasts and start your day off right. Experiment, explore, and enjoy the power of a delicious and nutritious breakfast.

CHAPTER 4

Lunch Recipes:

Remember that feeling? Mid-afternoon slump dragging you down, stomach growling like a hungry tiger, and your productivity nose diving faster than a forgotten sandwich in the back of the fridge? This chapter is your lunchbox superhero, here to rescue you from the dreaded hangry zone.

Forget boring brown bag lunches and sad desk salads. Here, we unlock a world of flavorful, satisfying, and easy-to-prepare lunch options that will fuel your body and mind, all while keeping your taste buds singing. Whether you're a time-pressed professional, a health-conscious foodie, or a busy parent juggling life's demands, this chapter has something for you.

Put an end to the lunchtime routine and the enraged monster once and for all! Lunchtime will no longer be a chore; be ready to discover tasty solutions, helpful hints, and motivational recipes. Get ready to attack the afternoon with a burst of energy and a satisfied stomach as we feed your day with flavor and nourish your body!

1. Grilled Chicken and Veggie Pita Pocket:

Ingredients:

- 1 boneless, skinless chicken breast, grilled and sliced
- 1/2 cup mixed roasted vegetables (bell peppers, onions, zucchini, etc.)
- 1 whole wheat pita pocket
- 1 tablespoon hummus (optional)
- Salt and pepper to taste

Instructions:

- Warm the pita pocket in the microwave or oven.
- Spread hummus inside the pita (optional).
- Fill the pita with sliced chicken and roasted vegetables.
- Season with salt and pepper to taste.

2. Black Bean and Corn Salad with Grilled Chicken:

Ingredients:

- 1 (15-ounce) can black beans, rinsed and drained
- 1 (15-ounce) can corn, drained
- 1 cup chopped tomatoes
- 4 ounces grilled chicken breast, cubed
- 1/4 cup chopped red onion
- 1/4 cup chopped fresh cilantro
- Simple vinaigrette dressing (recipe below)

Instructions:

- Combine all ingredients except dressing in a bowl.
- Toss with desired amount of vinaigrette dressing.
- Serve immediately.

Simple Vinaigrette:

- 2 tablespoons olive oil
- 1 tablespoon lemon juice
- 1 teaspoon Dijon mustard
- Salt and pepper to taste

3. Cauliflower Crust Pizza with Veggies:

Ingredients:

- 1 head cauliflower, riced and steamed
- 1 egg
- 1/4 cup grated Parmesan cheese
- 1/4 cup shredded mozzarella cheese
- 1/4 cup marinara sauce
- Your favorite chopped vegetables (bell peppers, onions, mushrooms, etc.)

Instructions:

- Preheat oven to 400°F (200°C).
- Combine riced cauliflower, egg, and Parmesan cheese in a bowl. Mix well.
- Spread cauliflower mixture onto a baking sheet lined with parchment paper, forming a pizza crust.
- Bake for 15 minutes.
- Top with marinara sauce and your favorite chopped vegetables.
- Sprinkle with mozzarella cheese.
- Bake for another 10-15 minutes, or until cheese is melted and vegetables are tender.

4. Open-Faced Tuna Melt with Avocado:

Ingredients:

- 1 can tuna, drained
- 1 tablespoon light mayonnaise
- 1 tablespoon finely chopped celery
- 1/4 cup diced avocado
- 1 whole-grain English muffin, toasted
- 1 slice low-fat cheese

Instructions:

- Combine tuna, mayonnaise, and celery in a bowl.
- Spread tuna mixture on one half of the toasted English muffin.
- Top with avocado and cheese.
- Broil for 2-3 minutes, or until cheese is melted and bubbly.

5. Turkey and Hummus Roll-Ups:

Ingredients:

- 4 slices low-carb tortillas
- 4 ounces sliced turkey deli meat
- 1/4 cup hummus
- 1 cup mixed baby greens
- 1/4 cup shredded carrots
- 1/4 cup chopped cucumber

Instructions:

- Spread hummus on each tortilla.
- Layer turkey, baby greens, carrots, and cucumber on top of hummus.
- Roll up tortillas tightly.
- Cut in half diagonally, if desired.

6. Greek-Style Salad with Grilled Shrimp:

Ingredients:

- 4 ounces grilled shrimp, peeled and deveined
- 2 cups romaine lettuce, chopped
- 1 cup cherry tomatoes, halved
- 1/2 cucumber, sliced
- 1/4 cup kalamata olives, pitted and halved
- 1/4 cup crumbled feta cheese
- Simple vinaigrette dressing (recipe above)

Instructions:

- Combine all ingredients except dressing in a bowl.
- Toss with desired amount of vinaigrette dressing.
- Serve immediately.

7. Chickpea and Kale Salad with Lemon Vinaigrette:

Ingredients:

- 1 (15-ounce) can chickpeas, rinsed and drained
- 4 cups chopped kale
- 1 cup cherry tomatoes, halved
- 1/4 cup chopped red onion
- 1/4 cup chopped fresh parsley
- Simple lemon vinaigrette dressing (recipe above)

Instructions:

- Combine all ingredients except dressing in a bowl.
- Toss with desired amount of lemon vinaigrette dressing.
- Serve immediately.

8. Turkey and Cheese Lettuce Wraps:

Ingredients:

- 4 large lettuce leaves (romaine, butter lettuce, etc.)
- 4 ounces sliced turkey deli meat
- 2 slices low-fat cheese
- 1/4 cup shredded carrots
- 1/4 cup chopped cucumber
- 1/4 cup chopped red onion (optional)
- Mustard (optional)

Instructions:

- Wash and dry the lettuce leaves.
- Layer turkey, cheese, carrots, cucumber, and red onion (if using) on each lettuce leaf.
- Spread a little mustard on the turkey (optional).
- Roll up the lettuce leaves tightly, starting from the bottom.

9. Curried Chicken Salad with Cashews:

Ingredients:

- 2 boneless, skinless chicken breasts, cooked and shredded
- 1/4 cup plain Greek yogurt
- 1 tablespoon mayonnaise
- 1 tablespoon curry powder
- 1/4 teaspoon ground ginger
- 1/4 cup chopped celery
- 1/4 cup chopped red onion
- 1/4 cup chopped cashews
- Salt and pepper to taste

Instructions:

- Combine all ingredients in a bowl and mix well.
- Serve on whole-wheat bread, crackers, or lettuce cups.

10. Salmon and Avocado Wrap:

Ingredients:

- 4 ounces grilled salmon, flaked
- 1/2 avocado, sliced
- 1 whole wheat tortilla
- 1 tablespoon plain Greek yogurt
- 1 teaspoon lemon juice
- 1/4 teaspoon dried dill
- Salt and pepper to taste

Instructions:

- Combine yogurt, lemon juice, and dill in a small bowl.
- Spread the yogurt mixture on the tortilla.
- Top with flaked salmon, avocado slices, and a sprinkle of salt and pepper.
- Roll up the tortilla tightly and enjoy!

Tips:

- Feel free to adjust the ingredients and seasonings in these recipes to your own taste.
- Get creative with toppings and garnishes for your salads and wraps.

- Pack leftovers in portion-controlled containers for quick and easy lunches on the go.

- Make a big batch of salad dressing or hummus on the weekend to save time during the week.

With these delicious and low-calorie lunch options, you can ditch the boring midday routine and fuel your body and mind for a productive and satisfying afternoon.

CHAPTER 5

Dinner Recipes

Imagine this: you've worked all day, the sun is going down, and your stomach is singing a familiar tune—it's time for dinner! When you factor in people who are finicky eaters, have busy schedules, and are often asking, **"What's for dinner?"** the once-magical evening meal can become more of a kitchen puzzle. Do not be afraid, fellow foodie! Here you will find a culinary map that will lead you to supper recipes that are easy to make, taste great, and take the stress out of mealtime.

Put away those daunting ingredients and intimidating recipes. Delicious meals that anybody can make using common ingredients and simple methods are celebrated here. This chapter contains recipes that are easy enough for a beginner to follow, as well as more advanced ones that will appeal to culinary experts searching for fresh ideas.

So, put down that takeout menu and get rid of the dinnertime dread. Embrace the joy of cooking and gathering around the table with loved ones. This chapter is your key to unlocking a world of flavorful, easy, and satisfying dinner creations that will make every mealtime a memorable occasion. **Let's get cooking.**

1. Grilled Steak with Roasted Asparagus:

Ingredients:

- 2 ribeye steaks (or your preferred cut)
- 1 bunch asparagus, trimmed
- Olive oil
- Salt and pepper
- Optional: Steak seasoning or marinade

Instructions:

- Preheat grill to medium-high heat.
- Brush asparagus with olive oil and season with salt and pepper. Arrange on a baking sheet and roast for 10-15 minutes, or until tender-crisp.
- Season steak with salt, pepper, and any desired seasoning. Grill for 3-4 minutes per side for medium-rare, or to your preferred doneness.
- Let steak rest for 5 minutes before slicing.
- Serve steak with roasted asparagus and enjoy!

2. Lemon Herb Baked Chicken with Roasted Potatoes:

Ingredients:

- 4 boneless, skinless chicken breasts
- 4 tablespoons olive oil
- 2 tablespoons lemon juice
- 1 tablespoon chopped fresh rosemary
- 1 tablespoon chopped fresh thyme
- 1 teaspoon garlic powder
- Salt and pepper
- 4 medium potatoes, chopped

Instructions:

- Preheat oven to 400°F (200°C).
- In a bowl, whisk together olive oil, lemon juice, rosemary, thyme, garlic powder, salt, and pepper.
- Coat chicken breasts generously with the lemon herb mixture.
- Place potatoes in a separate bowl and toss with olive oil, salt, and pepper.
- Spread potatoes on a baking sheet and arrange chicken breasts on top.

- Bake for 25-30 minutes, or until chicken is cooked through and potatoes are tender.
- Garnish with fresh herbs and enjoy!

3. Cauliflower Mac and Cheese with Chicken:

Ingredients:

- 1 head cauliflower, riced
- 1 pound boneless, skinless chicken breast, cooked and shredded
- 2 tablespoons butter
- 2 tablespoons flour
- 1 cup milk
- 1 cup shredded cheddar cheese
- 1/2 cup shredded mozzarella cheese
- Salt and pepper

Instructions:

- Preheat oven to 400°F (200°C).
- Steam cauliflower rice until tender.
- In a saucepan, melt butter over medium heat. Whisk in flour and cook for 1 minute. Slowly whisk in milk until a smooth sauce forms.
- Add cheddar cheese, mozzarella cheese, and salt and pepper to taste. Cook until cheese is melted and sauce is thickened.
- Stir in cooked cauliflower rice and chicken.

- Transfer mixture to a baking dish and top with additional mozzarella cheese, if desired.

- Bake for 15-20 minutes, or until golden brown and bubbly.

4. Grilled Salmon with Roasted Broccoli:

Ingredients:

- 2 salmon fillets
- 1 tablespoon olive oil
- 1 teaspoon dried dill
- 1/2 teaspoon garlic powder
- Salt and pepper
- 1 head broccoli, cut into florets

Instructions:

- Preheat grill to medium-high heat.
- Combine olive oil, dill, garlic powder, salt, and pepper in a bowl.
- Brush salmon fillets with the marinade.
- Grill for 4-5 minutes per side, or until cooked through.
- Meanwhile, toss broccoli florets with olive oil, salt, and pepper.
- Roast broccoli on a baking sheet for 10-15 minutes, or until tender-crisp.
- Serve salmon with roasted broccoli and enjoy!

5. Pork Tenderloin with Mashed Cauliflower:

Ingredients:

- 1 pork tenderloin
- 1 tablespoon olive oil
- Salt and pepper
- 1 head cauliflower, riced
- 1 clove garlic, minced
- 1/4 cup milk
- 2 tablespoons butter
- 1/4 cup grated Parmesan cheese
- Salt and pepper

Instructions:

- Preheat oven to 400°F (200°C).
- Season pork tenderloin with olive oil, salt, and pepper.
- Roast in the oven for 20-25 minutes, or until cooked through.
- While the pork cooks, steam cauliflower rice until tender.
- In a saucepan, heat butter over medium heat. Add garlic and cook for 1 minute.
- Stir in cauliflower rice and milk. Cook until heated through.

- Mash cauliflower rice with a fork or potato masher to desired consistency.
- Stir in Parmesan cheese, salt, and pepper to taste.
- Slice pork tenderloin and serve with mashed cauliflower.

6. Sesame Ginger Chicken with Vegetable Stir-Fry:

Ingredients:

- 1 pound boneless, skinless chicken breasts, sliced
- 2 tablespoons soy sauce
- 1 tablespoon rice vinegar
- 1 tablespoon sesame oil
- 1 tablespoon minced ginger
- 1 clove garlic, minced
- 1 teaspoon cornstarch
- 2 tablespoons vegetable oil
- 1 cup mixed vegetables (broccoli, carrots, bell peppers, etc.)
- 1/2 cup cooked rice

Instructions:

- Combine soy sauce, rice vinegar, sesame oil, ginger, garlic, and cornstarch in a bowl. Add chicken and marinate for 15 minutes.
- Heat vegetable oil in a large wok or skillet over high heat. Stir-fry chicken until cooked through, about 5 minutes. Remove from the pan and set aside.

- Add additional oil to the pan if needed. Add vegetables and stir-fry for 3-4 minutes, or until crisp-tender.
- Return chicken to the pan and toss with vegetables.
- Serve with cooked rice and enjoy!

7. Greek-Style Chicken and Vegetable Skewers:

Ingredients:

- 1 pound boneless, skinless chicken breast, cubed
- 1 bell pepper, cut into chunks
- 1 red onion, cut into chunks
- 1 zucchini, cut into chunks
- 1/4 cup olive oil
- 2 tablespoons lemon juice
- 1 tablespoon oregano
- 1 teaspoon garlic powder
- Salt and pepper

Instructions:

- Preheat grill to medium-high heat.
- Thread chicken, bell pepper, onion, and zucchini onto skewers.
- In a bowl, whisk together olive oil, lemon juice, oregano, garlic powder, salt, and pepper.
- Brush skewers with the marinade.
- Grill for 10-15 minutes, flipping occasionally, or until chicken is cooked through and vegetables are tender.
- Serve with a dollop of yogurt and crumbled feta cheese (optional).

8. Cabbage Roll-Ups with Ground Turkey:

Ingredients:

- 1 head cabbage, cored and leaves separated
- 1 pound ground turkey
- 1/2 cup cooked brown rice
- 1/2 cup diced onion
- 1/2 cup diced carrot
- 1/4 cup chopped celery
- 1 tablespoon tomato paste
- 1 teaspoon dried oregano
- 1/2 teaspoon garlic powder
- Salt and pepper
- 1 (14.5-ounce) can diced tomatoes, undrained

Instructions:

- Bring a large pot of salted water to a boil. Add cabbage leaves and cook for 2-3 minutes, or until softened. Remove from water and cool slightly.
- In a large bowl, combine ground turkey, brown rice, onion, carrot, celery, tomato paste, oregano, garlic powder, salt, and pepper. Mix well.
- Place a spoonful of the meat mixture on each cabbage leaf. Roll up the leaf and secure with a toothpick.

- Arrange roll-ups in a single layer in a baking dish.
- Pour diced tomatoes over roll-ups.
- Cover the baking dish with foil and bake at 375°F (190°C) for 30-35 minutes, or until cabbage is tender and turkey is cooked through.
- Serve warm and enjoy!

9. Baked Fish with Roasted Zucchini and Asparagus:

Ingredients:

- 2 fish fillets (cod, salmon, etc.)
- 1 tablespoon olive oil
- 1/2 teaspoon dried thyme
- 1/4 teaspoon garlic powder
- Salt and pepper
- 1 zucchini, sliced
- 1 bunch asparagus, trimmed

Instructions:

- Preheat oven to 400°F (200°C).
- Season fish fillets with olive oil, thyme, garlic powder, salt, and pepper.
- Arrange fish fillets in a baking dish.
- Toss zucchini and asparagus with olive oil, salt, and pepper.
- Arrange vegetables around the fish in the baking dish.
- Bake for 15-20 minutes, or until fish is cooked through and vegetables are tender.
- Serve with a lemon wedge and enjoy!

10. Spaghetti Squash with Meat Sauce:

Ingredients:

- 1 spaghetti squash
- 1 pound ground turkey
- 1 onion, diced
- 1 clove garlic, minced
- 1 (14.5-ounce) can diced tomatoes, undrained
- 1 tablespoon tomato paste
- 1 teaspoon dried oregano
- 1/2 teaspoon garlic powder
- Salt and pepper

Instructions:

- Preheat oven to 400°F (200°C).
- Cut spaghetti squash in half lengthwise and scoop out seeds.
- Place squash halves cut-side down in a baking dish and add 1/2 inch of water.
- Bake for 30-40 minutes, or until flesh is tender and easily shredded with a fork.
- Meanwhile, heat olive oil in a large skillet over medium heat.

- Add ground turkey and cook until browned, breaking it up with a spoon.
- Add onion and garlic to the skillet and cook for 5 minutes, or until softened.
- Stir in diced tomatoes, tomato paste, oregano, garlic powder, salt, and pepper. Bring to a simmer and cook for 10 minutes, stirring occasionally.
- Once squash is cooked, use a fork to shred the flesh into spaghetti-like strands.
- Transfer squash noodles to a large bowl and top with meat sauce.
- Enjoy garnished with grated Parmesan cheese or fresh herbs (optional).

Tips:

- Feel free to customize these recipes with your favorite ingredients and seasonings.
- Get creative with side dishes to complement each meal.
- Leftovers can be easily stored and repurposed for lunches or quick meals the next day.

With a little planning and these delicious recipes, you can enjoy satisfying and stress-free dinners all week long.

CHAPTER 6

Dessert Recipes

I love dessert. Warm, melt-in-your-mouth pastries, bursts of fruity taste, and luscious, chocolatey bliss come to mind at the very mention. It's the icing on the cake, the way your taste buds celebrate the end of a meal. But don't worry, sweets lover! Not only is this chapter all about sugary treats, but it's also about savoring each bite for its unique flavor, inventiveness, and delight.

Put out of your mind the daunting substances and laborious procedures. Discover a treasure trove of guilt-free dessert recipes that are simple to prepare, suitable for cooks of all experience levels, and guaranteed to fulfill your sweet cravings. This chapter is perfect for anyone, from seasoned bakers searching for new challenges to complete kitchen newbies in search of easy treats.

So, put down that store-bought ice cream and ditch the guilt! This chapter is your key to unlocking a world of simple, delicious, and satisfying dessert creations that will leave you and your loved ones wanting more. Get ready to dive into a world of sweetness, creativity, and pure dessert delight. Let's get baking!

1. Chocolate Chia Seed Pudding:

Ingredients:

- 1/4 cup chia seeds
- 1 cup almond milk
- 2 tablespoons cocoa powder
- 1 tablespoon maple syrup
- 1/2 teaspoon vanilla extract
- Pinch of salt (optional)
- Toppings (optional): fresh berries, nuts, shredded coconut, whipped cream

Instructions:

- In a bowl, whisk together chia seeds, almond milk, cocoa powder, maple syrup, vanilla extract, and salt (if using).
- Cover the bowl and refrigerate for at least 4 hours, or overnight, stirring occasionally.
- The pudding will thicken as the chia seeds absorb the liquid.
- Serve chilled, topped with your desired toppings.

2. Berry and Yogurt Parfait:

Ingredients:

- 1 cup plain Greek yogurt
- 1/2 cup mixed berries (fresh or frozen)
- 1/4 cup granola
- Optional toppings: honey, chopped nuts, chia seeds

Instructions:

- Layer yogurt, berries, and granola in a glass or parfait dish.
- Repeat the layers until the glass is full.
- Top with additional berries, granola, honey, nuts, or chia seeds (optional).

3. Dark Chocolate Bark with Almonds:

Ingredients:

- 8 ounces dark chocolate (at least 70% cocoa)
- 1/2 cup chopped almonds
- Pinch of sea salt (optional)

Instructions:

- Line a baking sheet with parchment paper.
- Melt the chocolate in a double boiler or microwave in short bursts, stirring until smooth.
- Pour the melted chocolate onto the prepared baking sheet and spread evenly.
- Sprinkle with chopped almonds and sea salt (optional).
- Refrigerate for at least 30 minutes, or until the chocolate is set.
- Break the bark into pieces and enjoy.

4. Banana and Peanut Butter Ice Cream:

Ingredients:

- 2 frozen bananas, peeled and chopped
- 2 tablespoons peanut butter
- 2 tablespoons almond milk (optional)

Instructions:

- Blend the frozen bananas in a high-powered blender until smooth and creamy.
- Add peanut butter and almond milk (if needed) and blend again until well combined.
- Serve immediately or freeze for a firmer consistency.

5. Mixed Berry Crumble:

Ingredients:

- 2 cups mixed berries (fresh or frozen)
- 1/4 cup almond flour
- 1/4 cup coconut flour
- 1/4 cup chopped nuts (pecans, almonds, walnuts)
- 1/4 cup melted coconut oil
- 1/4 cup maple syrup
- 1/4 teaspoon cinnamon

Instructions:

- Preheat oven to 375°F (190°C).
- In a bowl, combine almond flour, coconut flour, chopped nuts, and cinnamon.
- Stir in melted coconut oil and maple syrup until a crumbly mixture forms.
- Spread half of the crumble mixture on a baking sheet.
- Top with mixed berries.
- Sprinkle remaining crumble mixture over the berries.
- Bake for 20-25 minutes, or until the crumble is golden brown and the berries are bubbly.
- Serve warm or at room temperature.

6. Pumpkin and Spice Chia Pudding:

Ingredients:

- 1/4 cup chia seeds
- 1 cup unsweetened almond milk
- 1/2 cup pumpkin puree
- 1 tablespoon maple syrup
- 1/2 teaspoon ground cinnamon
- 1/4 teaspoon ground ginger
- 1/4 teaspoon ground nutmeg
- Pinch of salt

Instructions:

- In a bowl, whisk together chia seeds, almond milk, pumpkin puree, maple syrup, spices, and salt.
- Cover the bowl and refrigerate for at least 4 hours, or overnight, stirring occasionally.
- Serve chilled, topped with additional pumpkin puree, chopped nuts, or seeds (optional).

7. Grilled Peach and Greek Yogurt Sundae:

Ingredients:

- 2 ripe peaches, halved and pitted
- Olive oil
- 1/2 cup plain Greek yogurt
- Toppings (optional): honey, chopped nuts, granola, berries

Instructions:

- Brush the peach halves with olive oil.
- Grill the peaches over medium heat until slightly softened and browned, about 2-3 minutes per side.
- Top the grilled peaches with Greek yogurt and your desired toppings.

8. Strawberry and Almond Milk Smoothie:

Ingredients:

- 1 cup frozen strawberries
- 1 cup almond milk
- 1 tablespoon honey (optional)
- Vanilla extract to taste

Instructions:

- Blend all ingredients together in a blender until smooth and creamy.
- Adjust sweetness to taste with additional honey or vanilla extract.
- Serve immediately.

9. Blueberry and Almond Flour Crustless Pie:

Ingredients:

- 2 cups fresh blueberries
- 1/2 cup almond flour
- 1/4 cup coconut flour
- 1/4 cup melted coconut oil
- 1/4 cup maple syrup
- 1/4 teaspoon cinnamon

Instructions:

- Preheat oven to 375°F (190°C).
- In a bowl, combine almond flour, coconut flour, and cinnamon.
- Stir in melted coconut oil and maple syrup until a crumbly mixture forms.
- Press half of the crumble mixture into the bottom of a pie dish or baking sheet.
- Spread blueberries evenly over the crust.
- Sprinkle remaining crumble mixture over the berries.
- Bake for 20-25 minutes, or until the crumble is golden brown and the berries are bubbly.
- Cool slightly before serving.

10. Chocolate and Avocado Mousse:

Ingredients:

- 2 ripe avocados, peeled and pitted
- 1/2 cup unsweetened cocoa powder
- 1/4 cup maple syrup
- 1 tablespoon milk (dairy or non-dairy)
- 1 teaspoon vanilla extract
- Pinch of salt

Instructions:

- In a food processor, blend together avocados, cocoa powder, maple syrup, milk, vanilla extract, and salt until smooth and creamy.
- Taste and adjust sweetness or cocoa powder as desired.
- Divide the mousse between serving cups or glasses.
- Refrigerate for at least 30 minutes before serving.
- Top with fresh berries, whipped cream, or shaved chocolate (optional).

These are just basic recipes! Feel free to experiment with different ingredients and toppings to create your own unique and delicious desserts. Enjoy!

CHAPTER 7

Satisfying Salads and Soups

Lettuce celebrates! Salads that were formerly considered rabbit chow are now considered vibrant and healthy. Indulge in fulfilling salads and heartwarming soups as this chapter takes you on a lively tour of their culinary wonderland.

Leave the flimsy greens and watery broths at the door. Indulge in flavor explosions bursting at the seams with protein powerhouses, colorful sauces, and fresh, seasonal ingredients. Whether you're a soup skeptic in search of something warm and comforting or a salad enthusiast looking for new ideas, this chapter has something for everyone.

So, put down that wilted lettuce and ditch the canned soup routine. Embrace the versatility and flavor potential of these culinary gems. Explore the recipes, unleash your inner chef, and experience the joy of creating nourishing and satisfying bowls of goodness that will leave you feeling energized, inspired, and ready to conquer your day (or night)! **Let's get cookin'!**

Salads:

1. Chicken and Avocado Caesar Salad:

Ingredients:

- 1 boneless, skinless chicken breast, grilled and sliced
- 1/2 avocado, sliced
- 2 cups romaine lettuce, chopped
- 1/4 cup grated Parmesan cheese
- 1/4 cup homemade low-carb Caesar dressing (recipe below)

Instructions:

- Combine all ingredients in a bowl and toss to coat.
- Serve immediately.

Low-Carb Caesar Dressing:

- 1/4 cup mayonnaise
- 2 tablespoons plain Greek yogurt
- 1 tablespoon lemon juice
- 1 tablespoon Dijon mustard
- 1 clove garlic, minced
- 1/4 teaspoon anchovy paste (optional)
- 1/4 teaspoon dried oregano
- 1/4 teaspoon black pepper

- Salt to taste

Instructions:

- Whisk all ingredients together until smooth.
- Use immediately or store in an airtight container in the refrigerator for up to 3 days.

2. Salmon and Spinach Salad with Lemon Vinaigrette:

Ingredients:

- 4 ounces grilled salmon, flaked
- 4 cups fresh spinach
- 1/2 cup cherry tomatoes, halved
- 1/4 cup red onion, thinly sliced
- 1/4 cup crumbled feta cheese
- Lemon Vinaigrette (recipe below)

Instructions:

- Combine all ingredients in a bowl and toss to coat.
- Drizzle with desired amount of lemon vinaigrette.
- Serve immediately.

Lemon Vinaigrette:

- 3 tablespoons olive oil
- 2 tablespoons lemon juice
- 1 tablespoon Dijon mustard
- 1/2 teaspoon honey
- 1/4 teaspoon dried oregano
- Salt and pepper to taste

Instructions:

- Whisk all ingredients together until well combined.
- Store in an airtight container in the refrigerator for up to 1 week.

3. Taco Salad with Ground Turkey:

Ingredients:

- 1 pound ground turkey, browned and seasoned
- 2 cups romaine lettuce, chopped
- 1 cup cherry tomatoes, halved
- 1/2 cup black beans, rinsed and drained
- 1/4 cup shredded cheddar cheese
- 1/4 cup sliced avocado
- Homemade salsa dressing (recipe below)

Instructions:

- Combine all ingredients in a bowl and toss to coat.
- Drizzle with desired amount of salsa dressing.
- Serve immediately.

Salsa Dressing:

- 1 cup salsa of your choice
- 2 tablespoons plain Greek yogurt
- 1 tablespoon lime juice
- 1/4 teaspoon cumin
- Salt and pepper to taste

Instructions:

- Blend all ingredients together until smooth.
- Serve immediately or store in an airtight container in the refrigerator for up to 3 days.

4. Greek Salad with Grilled Chicken:

Ingredients:

- 4 ounces grilled chicken breast, sliced
- 4 cups romaine lettuce, chopped
- 1 cup cherry tomatoes, halved
- 1/2 cup cucumber, sliced
- 1/4 cup kalamata olives, pitted and halved
- 1/4 cup crumbled feta cheese
- Simple vinaigrette (recipe below)

Instructions:

- Combine all ingredients in a bowl and toss to coat.
- Drizzle with desired amount of vinaigrette.
- Serve immediately.

Simple Vinaigrette:

- 3 tablespoons olive oil
- 2 tablespoons red wine vinegar
- 1 teaspoon Dijon mustard
- Salt and pepper to taste

Instructions:

- Whisk all ingredients together until well combined.

- Store in an airtight container in the refrigerator for up to 1 week.

5. Chicken and Strawberry Salad with Poppy Seed Dressing:

Ingredients:

- 4 ounces grilled chicken breast, sliced
- 1 cup fresh strawberries, sliced
- 2 cups mixed greens
- 1/4 cup crumbled blue cheese
- 1/4 cup homemade low-carb poppy seed dressing (recipe below)

Instructions:

- Combine all ingredients in a bowl and toss to coat.
- Drizzle with desired amount of poppy seed dressing.
- Serve immediately.

Low-Carb Poppy Seed Dressing:

- 1/4 cup olive oil
- 2 tablespoons apple cider vinegar
- 1 tablespoon Dijon mustard
- 1 tablespoon honey
- 1 teaspoon poppy seeds
- Salt and pepper to taste

Instructions:

- Whisk all ingredients together until well combined.
- Store in an airtight container in the refrigerator for up to 1 week.

Soups:

1. Chicken and Vegetable Soup:

Ingredients:

- 1 pound boneless, skinless chicken breasts
- 8 cups chicken broth
- 4 carrots, chopped
- 2 celery stalks, chopped
- 1 onion, chopped
- 4 cups spinach, chopped
- Salt and pepper to taste

Instructions:

- In a large pot, combine chicken breasts and chicken broth. Bring to a boil, then reduce heat and simmer for 15 minutes, or until chicken is cooked through.
- Remove chicken from the pot and shred with two forks. Set aside.
- Add carrots, celery, and onion to the pot and simmer for 5 minutes, or until softened.
- Stir in spinach and cook until wilted.
- Return shredded chicken to the pot and season with salt and pepper to taste.
- Serve hot.

2. Creamy Cauliflower Soup:

Ingredients:

- 1 head cauliflower, chopped
- 4 cups chicken broth
- 1 onion, chopped
- 2 cloves garlic, minced
- 1/4 cup heavy cream
- Salt and pepper to taste

Instructions:

- In a large pot, melt butter over medium heat. Add onion and garlic and cook until softened, about 5 minutes.
- Add cauliflower and chicken broth and bring to a boil. Reduce heat and simmer for 15 minutes, or until cauliflower is tender.
- Puree soup with an immersion blender or in batches in a blender until smooth.
- Stir in heavy cream and season with salt and pepper to taste.
- Serve hot, garnished with fresh herbs or a swirl of cream (optional).

3. Turkey Chili:

Ingredients:

- 1 pound ground turkey, browned
- 1 onion, chopped
- 2 cloves garlic, minced
- 1 (28-ounce) can crushed tomatoes
- 1 (15-ounce) can kidney beans, drained and rinsed
- 1 (15-ounce) can black beans, drained and rinsed
- 1 (15-ounce) can corn, drained
- 1 tablespoon chili powder
- 1 teaspoon cumin
- 1/2 teaspoon smoked paprika
- Salt and pepper to taste

Instructions:

- In a large pot, brown ground turkey over medium heat. Drain off any excess fat.
- Add onion and garlic to the pot and cook until softened, about 5 minutes.
- Stir in crushed tomatoes, kidney beans, black beans, corn, chili powder, cumin, and smoked paprika. Bring to a boil, then reduce heat and simmer for 30 minutes, or until flavors have melded.

- Season with salt and pepper to taste.

- Serve hot, garnished with your favorite toppings such as avocado, sour cream, shredded cheese, and chopped onion.

4. Creamy Mushroom Soup:

Ingredients:

- 1 pound mushrooms, sliced
- 4 cups chicken broth
- 1 onion, chopped
- 2 cloves garlic, minced
- 1/4 cup heavy cream
- Salt and pepper to taste

Instructions:

- In a large pot, melt butter over medium heat. Add onion and garlic and cook until softened, about 5 minutes.
- Add mushrooms and cook until softened and browned, about 10 minutes.
- Add chicken broth and bring to a boil. Reduce heat and simmer for 15 minutes, or until mushrooms are tender.
- Puree soup with an immersion blender or in batches in a blender until smooth.
- Stir in heavy cream and season with salt and pepper to taste.
- Serve hot, garnished with fresh herbs or a swirl of cream (optional).

5. Cabbage and White Bean Soup:

Ingredients:

- 1 head cabbage, chopped
- 1 (15-ounce) can cannellini beans, drained and rinsed
- 4 cups vegetable broth
- 1 onion, chopped
- 2 cloves garlic, minced
- 1 tablespoon olive oil
- Salt and pepper to taste

Instructions:

- In a large pot, heat olive oil over medium heat. Add onion and garlic and cook until softened, about 5 minutes.
- Add cabbage and vegetable broth and bring to a boil. Reduce heat and simmer for 15 minutes, or until cabbage is tender.
- Stir in cannellini beans and season with salt and pepper to taste.
- Serve hot, garnished with fresh herbs or a drizzle of olive oil (optional).

Enjoy these delicious and satisfying salads and soups!

Tips:

- Feel free to adjust the ingredients and seasonings in these recipes to your own taste.
- Get creative with toppings and garnishes for your salads

CHAPTER 8

Low-Carb Side Dishes

Embracing a low-carb lifestyle doesn't have to mean sacrificing flavor or variety. In fact, it can be an exciting opportunity to explore new ingredients, discover hidden gems of the vegetable world, and unlock a world of side dishes that are both delicious and health-conscious.

Gone are the days of bland steamed broccoli and watery green beans. Here, we ditch the limitations and celebrate a vibrant collection of low-carb side dishes that will complement your meals, tantalize your taste buds, and leave you feeling satisfied and energized.

Whether you're a seasoned low-carb veteran or just dipping your toes into this dietary approach, this chapter is your treasure trove of delicious inspiration.

1. Roasted Cauliflower with Parmesan Cheese:

Ingredients:

- 1 head cauliflower, cut into florets
- 1 tablespoon olive oil
- 1/2 teaspoon dried oregano
- 1/4 teaspoon salt
- 1/4 teaspoon black pepper
- 1/4 cup grated Parmesan cheese

Instructions:

- Preheat oven to 400°F (200°C).
- Toss cauliflower florets with olive oil, oregano, salt, and pepper.
- Spread on a baking sheet and roast for 20-25 minutes, or until tender and lightly browned.
- Sprinkle with Parmesan cheese and serve immediately.

2. Sautéed Spinach with Garlic:

Ingredients:

- 10 ounces fresh spinach, washed and dried
- 1 tablespoon olive oil
- 2 cloves garlic, minced
- Salt and pepper to taste

Instructions:

- Heat olive oil in a large skillet over medium heat.
- Add garlic and cook for 30 seconds, until fragrant.
- Add spinach and cook, stirring constantly, until wilted.
- Season with salt and pepper to taste.
- Serve immediately.

3. Zucchini and Yellow Squash Ribbon Salad:

Ingredients:

- 1 medium zucchini
- 1 medium yellow squash
- 2 tablespoons olive oil
- 1 tablespoon lemon juice
- 1/4 teaspoon dried oregano
- Salt and pepper to taste
- Chopped fresh herbs (optional: parsley, basil, dill)

Instructions:

- Using a spiralizer or mandoline, create thin ribbons from the zucchini and yellow squash.
- In a bowl, whisk together olive oil, lemon juice, oregano, salt, and pepper.
- Toss the zucchini and squash ribbons with the dressing.
- Garnish with chopped fresh herbs (optional) and serve immediately.

4. Roasted Brussels Sprouts with Bacon:

Ingredients:

- 1 pound Brussels sprouts, trimmed and halved
- 2 tablespoons olive oil
- 1/2 teaspoon salt
- 1/4 teaspoon black pepper
- 2 slices bacon, chopped

Instructions:

- Preheat oven to 400°F (200°C).
- Toss Brussels sprouts with olive oil, salt, and pepper.
- Spread on a baking sheet and roast for 20-25 minutes, or until tender and browned.
- In the last 5 minutes of cooking, add chopped bacon and cook until crispy.
- Serve immediately.

5. Creamy Cabbage and Bacon:

Ingredients:

- 1 head cabbage, shredded
- 2 slices bacon, chopped
- 1 tablespoon olive oil
- 1/4 cup chicken broth
- 1/4 cup heavy cream
- 1/4 teaspoon salt
- 1/4 teaspoon black pepper

Instructions:

- Heat olive oil in a large skillet over medium heat.
- Add bacon and cook until crispy. Remove with a slotted spoon and set aside.
- Add shredded cabbage to the pan and cook for 5 minutes, stirring occasionally.
- Pour in chicken broth and heavy cream.
- Season with salt and pepper and bring to a simmer.
- Reduce heat and cook for 5-7 minutes, or until cabbage is tender and sauce thickens slightly.
- Stir in reserved bacon and serve immediately.

6. Broccoli Slaw with Lemon Vinaigrette:

Ingredients:

- 1 head broccoli, florets and stem thinly sliced
- 1 carrot, grated
- 1/4 cup olive oil
- 2 tablespoons lemon juice
- 1 tablespoon Dijon mustard
- 1 teaspoon honey
- 1/4 teaspoon salt
- 1/4 teaspoon black pepper
- Chopped fresh herbs (optional: parsley, chives)

Instructions:

- Combine broccoli florets, stem, and grated carrot in a large bowl.
- In a separate bowl, whisk together olive oil, lemon juice, Dijon mustard, honey, salt, and pepper.
- Pour the dressing over the broccoli mixture and toss to coat.
- Garnish with chopped fresh herbs (optional) and serve immediately.

7. Green Beans with Pecans and Bacon:

Ingredients:

- 1 pound fresh green beans, trimmed and halved
- 2 tablespoons olive oil
- 2 cloves garlic, minced
- 1/4 cup chopped pecans
- 2 slices bacon, chopped
- Salt and pepper to taste

Instructions:

- Heat olive oil in a large skillet over medium heat.
- Add garlic and cook for 30 seconds, until fragrant.
- Add green beans and cook for 5-7 minutes, or until crisp-tender.
- Add chopped pecans and bacon and cook for an additional 2-3 minutes, until bacon is crispy.
- Season with salt and pepper to taste.
- Serve immediately.

8. Cauliflower Rice with Ginger and Garlic:

Ingredients:

- 1 head cauliflower, riced
- 1 tablespoon olive oil
- 1 clove garlic, minced
- 1 teaspoon grated ginger
- 1/4 cup chicken broth
- Salt and pepper to taste
- Chopped green onions (optional)

Instructions:

- Heat olive oil in a large skillet over medium heat.
- Add garlic and ginger and cook for 30 seconds, until fragrant.
- Add riced cauliflower and cook for 5-7 minutes, stirring occasionally.
- Pour in chicken broth and cook for an additional 2-3 minutes, or until liquid is absorbed.
- Season with salt and pepper to taste.
- Garnish with chopped green onions (optional) and serve immediately.

9. Spaghetti Squash with Marinara Sauce:

Ingredients:

- 1 spaghetti squash
- 1 tablespoon olive oil
- Salt and pepper to taste
- Marinara sauce of your choice

Instructions:

- Preheat oven to 400°F (200°C).
- Cut spaghetti squash in half lengthwise and remove seeds.
- Brush the flesh with olive oil and season with salt and pepper.
- Place cut-side down on a baking sheet and roast for 40-45 minutes, or until flesh is tender and easily pulls away with a fork.
- Using a fork, shred the flesh into spaghetti-like strands.
- Top with your favorite marinara sauce and serve immediately.

10. Creamed Spinach with Parmesan Cheese:

Ingredients:

- 10 ounces fresh spinach, washed and dried
- 1 tablespoon butter
- 1 tablespoon flour
- 1 cup milk
- 1/4 cup grated Parmesan cheese
- 1/4 teaspoon salt
- 1/4 teaspoon black pepper
- Nutmeg (optional)

Instructions:

- Melt butter in a large skillet over medium heat.
- Whisk in flour and cook for 1 minute.
- Slowly whisk in milk and bring to a simmer.
- Add spinach and cook, stirring constantly, until wilted.
- Stir in Parmesan cheese, salt, pepper, and nutmeg (optional).
- Serve immediately.

Remember, these are just a starting point! Feel free to experiment with different herbs, spices, and toppings to personalize these recipes and create your own low-carb side dish favorites. Enjoy!

CHAPTER 9

Tips for sustaining weight loss and avoiding weight regain

Congratulations! You've reached your weight loss goal. You feel fantastic, your clothes fit better, and your energy levels are soaring. But now what? How do you prevent the dreaded rebound and maintain your success? Don't worry, champion, this isn't the end of your journey, it's just the beginning of a new chapter: sustainable weight management.

Think of it like training for a marathon. You wouldn't stop running after crossing the finish line, would you? You'd maintain your fitness routine in a slightly different way, enjoying the journey and reaping the long-term benefits. In the same way, sustainable weight management involves shifting your mindset from achieving a goal to adopting healthy habits for life.

Here are some key tips to guide you on this exciting new chapter:

1. Reframe Your Mindset:

Instead of constantly focusing on "restriction" and "dieting," cultivate a positive relationship with food based on nourishment and mindful choices. Embrace a sustainable lifestyle, not just a temporary diet. Celebrate your non-scale victories and focus on the overall health benefits you're experiencing.

2. Don't Demonize Food:

Remember, food is not the enemy. Every food has its place in a balanced diet. Instead of labelling foods as "good" or "bad," learn about portion control and indulge in your favorite treats occasionally. Don't deprive yourself and risk triggering cravings and binge eating.

3. Find Your Food Freedom:

Discover the foods that work for you and your body. Explore new recipes, find healthy alternatives you enjoy, and prepare your own meals more often. This gives you control over ingredients and portion sizes, and fosters a sense of empowerment.

4. Stay Active, Not Just Active:

Exercise isn't just about burning calories; it's about moving your body in ways you enjoy. Find activities you genuinely like, be it dancing, swimming, hiking, or team sports. Make movement a regular part of your life, not just a chore to tick off your list.

5. Sleep Well, Stress Less:

Chronic sleep deprivation and stress can wreak havoc on your hormones, leading to increased cravings and weight gain. Prioritize quality sleep by establishing a regular sleep schedule and creating a relaxing bedtime routine. Manage stress through healthy coping mechanisms like meditation, yoga, or spending time in nature.

6. Build a Support System:

Surround yourself with people who support your journey. Join a supportive community, seek guidance from a registered dietitian or weight management coach, and confide in trusted friends and family who understand your goals.

7. Embrace Imperfections:

There will be slip-ups and setbacks. The key is not to dwell on them or use them as an excuse to give up. Forgive yourself, learn from the experience, and get back on track. Remember, progress, not perfection, is the key.

8. Celebrate, Reflect, Adapt:

Celebrate your non-scale victories, big and small. Reflect on your journey and the strategies that worked for you. As your life evolves, be willing to adapt your approach to maintain a healthy lifestyle that fits your needs and preferences.

This is not just about weight loss; it's about creating a healthier, happier, and more fulfilling life. By incorporating these tips and embracing a sustainable approach, you can confidently step into the next chapter of your journey, ensuring long-term success and vibrant well-being.

CONCLUSION

Bon appétit, and Beyond!

Well, my friend, we've reached the end of this delicious adventure. From mouthwatering main courses to satisfying desserts, we've explored a world of culinary possibilities. But remember, this cookbook is just the beginning. It's not simply a collection of recipes, but a springboard for your own culinary creativity.

Think of these pages as the starting point for countless delicious journeys. Experiment with flavors, swap ingredients, and personalize each dish to suit your taste buds and dietary needs. Let your cooking become an expression of your individuality and a source of joy for yourself and those you love.

But food is more than just sustenance; it's a way to connect with loved ones, celebrate special occasions, and create lasting memories. Remember the laughter shared over a perfectly cooked meal, the warmth of a family dinner gathered around the table, the excitement of trying a new cuisine. Let these experiences fuel your passion for cooking and inspire you to continue exploring the endless possibilities of the culinary world.

So, dear reader, close this book, not as an ending, but as a new beginning. Go forth, armed with delicious inspiration and a spirit of adventure. Share your love of food with others, create memories that will last a lifetime, and most importantly, savor the journey.

And remember, if you ever find yourself stuck in a culinary rut, or simply needing a spark of inspiration, pick up this book again. These pages hold not just recipes, but a reminder of the joy, connection, and satisfaction that food can bring.

Happy cooking, and happy eating!

P.S. Don't forget to share your culinary creations with me! Use the hashtag #YourCookbookAdventure and let's see what deliciousness you concoct!

Meal

PLANNER

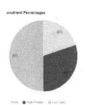

WEEK :

DATE :

MONDAY

B

L

D

S

TUESDAY

B

L

D

S

WEDNESDAY

B

L

D

S

THURSDAY

B

L

D

S

FRIDAY

B

L

D

S

SATURDAY

B

L

D

S

Meal

PLANNER

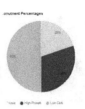

onutrient Percentages

Yose ● High-Protein @ Low-Carb

WEEK :

DATE :

MONDAY

B

L

D

S

THURSDAY

B

L

D

S

TUESDAY

B

L

D

S

FRIDAY

B

L

D

S

WEDNESDAY

B

L

D

S

SATURDAY

B

L

D

S

Meal

PLANNER

WEEK :

DATE :

MONDAY

B

L

D

S

TUESDAY

B

L

D

S

WEDNESDAY

B

L

D

S

THURSDAY

B

L

D

S

FRIDAY

B

L

D

S

SATURDAY

B

L

D

S

Meal

PLANNER

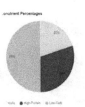

onutrient Percentages

WEEK :   **DATE :**

MONDAY

B

L

D

S

TUESDAY

B

L

D

S

WEDNESDAY

B

L

D

S

THURSDAY

B

L

D

S

FRIDAY

B

L

D

S

SATURDAY

B

L

D

S

Meal
PLANNER

onutrient Percentages

WEEK :

DATE :

MONDAY	THURSDAY
B	B
L	L
D	D
S	S

TUESDAY	FRIDAY
B	B
L	L
D	D
S	S

WEDNESDAY	SATURDAY
B	B
L	L
D	D
S	S

Meal

PLANNER

onutrient Percentages

High-Protein · Low-Carb

WEEK : _____   **DATE :** _____

MONDAY

B	
L	
D	
S	

TUESDAY

B	
L	
D	
S	

WEDNESDAY

B	
L	
D	
S	

THURSDAY

B	
L	
D	
S	

FRIDAY

B	
L	
D	
S	

SATURDAY

B	
L	
D	
S	

Meal

PLANNER

onutrient Percentages

Foods · High Protein · Low Carb

WEEK :

DATE :

MONDAY

B

L

D

S

THURSDAY

B

L

D

S

TUESDAY

B

L

D

S

FRIDAY

B

L

D

S

WEDNESDAY

B

L

D

S

SATURDAY

B

L

D

S

Meal

PLANNER

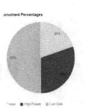

onutrient Percentages

WEEK :

DATE :

MONDAY

B

L

D

S

THURSDAY

B

L

D

S

TUESDAY

B

L

D

S

FRIDAY

B

L

D

S

WEDNESDAY

B

L

D

S

SATURDAY

B

L

D

S

Meal
PLANNER

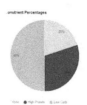

onstrient Percentages

High Protein   Low Carb

WEEK :   DATE :

MONDAY   **THURSDAY**

B   B
L   L
D   D
S   S

TUESDAY   **FRIDAY**

B   B
L   L
D   D
S   S

WEDNESDAY   **SATURDAY**

B   B
L   L
D   D
S   S

Meal
PLANNER

WEEK : _____

DATE : _____

MONDAY

B

L

D

S

TUESDAY

B

L

D

S

WEDNESDAY

B

L

D

S

THURSDAY

B

L

D

S

FRIDAY

B

L

D

S

SATURDAY

B

L

D

S

Meal

PLANNER

onutrient Percentages

Vnole ● High Protein ● Low Carb

WEEK :

DATE :

MONDAY

B

L

D

S

TUESDAY

B

L

D

S

WEDNESDAY

B

L

D

S

THURSDAY

B

L

D

S

FRIDAY

B

L

D

S

SATURDAY

B

L

D

S

Meal

PLANNER

onutrient Percentages

WEEK :

DATE :

MONDAY

B	
L	
D	
S	

THURSDAY

B	
L	
D	
S	

TUESDAY

B	
L	
D	
S	

FRIDAY

B	
L	
D	
S	

WEDNESDAY

B	
L	
D	
S	

SATURDAY

B	
L	
D	
S	

Meal
PLANNER

onutrient Percentages

WEEK : _____

DATE : _____

MONDAY		THURSDAY	
B		B	
L		L	
D		D	
S		S	

TUESDAY		FRIDAY	
B		B	
L		L	
D		D	
S		S	

WEDNESDAY		SATURDAY	
B		B	
L		L	
D		D	
S		S	

Meal

PLANNER

Macronutrient Percentages

WEEK :

DATE :

MONDAY

B

L

D

S

TUESDAY

B

L

D

S

WEDNESDAY

B

L

D

S

THURSDAY

B

L

D

S

FRIDAY

B

L

D

S

SATURDAY

B

L

D

S

Meal

PLANNER

onutrient Percentages

WEEK :

DATE :

MONDAY

B

L

D

S

TUESDAY

B

L

D

S

WEDNESDAY

B

L

D

S

THURSDAY

B

L

D

S

FRIDAY

B

L

D

S

SATURDAY

B

L

D

S

Meal

PLANNER

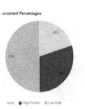

WEEK :

DATE :

MONDAY

B

L

D

S

TUESDAY

B

L

D

S

WEDNESDAY

B

L

D

S

THURSDAY

B

L

D

S

FRIDAY

B

L

D

S

SATURDAY

B

L

D

S

Meal

PLANNER

onutrient Percentages

Work ● High-Protein ● Low Carb

WEEK :

DATE :

MONDAY

B

L

D

S

TUESDAY

B

L

D

S

WEDNESDAY

B

L

D

S

THURSDAY

B

L

D

S

FRIDAY

B

L

D

S

SATURDAY

B

L

D

S

Meal

PLANNER

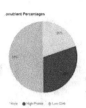

onutrient Percentages

WEEK :

DATE :

MONDAY

B

L

D

S

TUESDAY

B

L

D

S

WEDNESDAY

B

L

D

S

THURSDAY

B

L

D

S

FRIDAY

B

L

D

S

SATURDAY

B

L

D

S

Meal

PLANNER

Macronutrient Percentages

Whole · High-Protein · Low-Carb

WEEK :

DATE :

MONDAY

B

L

D

S

TUESDAY

B

L

D

S

WEDNESDAY

B

L

D

S

THURSDAY

B

L

D

S

FRIDAY

B

L

D

S

SATURDAY

B

L

D

S

Meal

PLANNER

onutrient Percentages

High Protein   Low Carb

WEEK :

DATE :

MONDAY

B

L

D

S

THURSDAY

B

L

D

S

TUESDAY

B

L

D

S

FRIDAY

B

L

D

S

WEDNESDAY

B

L

D

S

SATURDAY

B

L

D

S

Meal
PLANNER

Onutrient Percentages

WEEK :

DATE :

MONDAY

B

L

D

S

TUESDAY

B

L

D

S

WEDNESDAY

B

L

D

S

THURSDAY

B

L

D

S

FRIDAY

B

L

D

S

SATURDAY

B

L

D

S

Meal

PLANNER

onutrient Percentages

WEEK :

DATE :

MONDAY

B

L

D

S

THURSDAY

B

L

D

S

TUESDAY

B

L

D

S

FRIDAY

B

L

D

S

WEDNESDAY

B

L

D

S

SATURDAY

B

L

D

S

Meal

PLANNER

onutrient Percentages

WEEK : _____

DATE : _____

MONDAY

B

L

D

S

TUESDAY

B

L

D

S

WEDNESDAY

B

L

D

S

THURSDAY

B

L

D

S

FRIDAY

B

L

D

S

SATURDAY

B

L

D

S

Meal

PLANNER

onutrient Percentages

WEEK :

DATE :

MONDAY

B

L

D

S

TUESDAY

B

L

D

S

WEDNESDAY

B

L

D

S

THURSDAY

B

L

D

S

FRIDAY

B

L

D

S

SATURDAY

B

L

D

S

Meal

PLANNER

onutrient Percentages

WEEK : _____

DATE : _____

MONDAY

B

L

D

S

TUESDAY

B

L

D

S

WEDNESDAY

B

L

D

S

THURSDAY

B

L

D

S

FRIDAY

B

L

D

S

SATURDAY

B

L

D

S

Meal

PLANNER

WEEK :

DATE :

MONDAY

B

L

D

S

TUESDAY

B

L

D

S

WEDNESDAY

B

L

D

S

THURSDAY

B

L

D

S

FRIDAY

B

L

D

S

SATURDAY

B

L

D

S

Meal
PLANNER

WEEK :

DATE :

MONDAY

B

L

D

S

TUESDAY

B

L

D

S

WEDNESDAY

B

L

D

S

THURSDAY

B

L

D

S

FRIDAY

B

L

D

S

SATURDAY

B

L

D

S

Meal

PLANNER

.onutrient Percentages

WEEK :

DATE :

MONDAY

B

L

D

S

TUESDAY

B

L

D

S

WEDNESDAY

B

L

D

S

THURSDAY

B

L

D

S

FRIDAY

B

L

D

S

SATURDAY

B

L

D

S

Meal
PLANNER

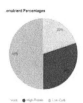

onutrient Percentages

WEEK :

DATE :

MONDAY

B

L

D

S

TUESDAY

B

L

D

S

WEDNESDAY

B

L

D

S

THURSDAY

B

L

D

S

FRIDAY

B

L

D

S

SATURDAY

B

L

D

S

Meal

PLANNER

Macronutrient Percentages

WEEK :

DATE :

MONDAY

B

L

D

S

TUESDAY

B

L

D

S

WEDNESDAY

B

L

D

S

THURSDAY

B

L

D

S

FRIDAY

B

L

D

S

SATURDAY

B

L

D

S

www.ingramcontent.com/pod-product-compliance
Lightning Source LLC
LaVergne TN
LVHW010219300425
809993LV00020B/302

* 9 7 9 8 8 8 3 8 9 5 2 7 1 *